Entrepreneurship And Business Life Coach Certification

SADANAND PUJARI

Published by SADANAND PUJARI, 2023.

Table of Contents

Copyright

Entrepreneurship And Business Life Coach Certification

First Edition: Dec 2023

Book Design by **SADANAND PUJARI**

About

Are you ready to learn and teach proven entrepreneurship skills?

Do you want to coach your clients towards entrepreneurship so that they can make money doing what they love, start a business, get more clients, or take their business to the next level?

Become a Certified Entrepreneurship and Business Coach!

Self-employment through Entrepreneurship is the ultimate form of self-empowerment, and by coaching clients to create a thriving business, you are handing them the key to their freedom to determine their destiny and fulfill their life's purpose.

This program is designed for life coaches who want to work with those that want to improve their entrepreneurship skills such as or solopreneurs, such as contractors, independent practitioners, life coaches, or small business owners with only a handful of employees. These can be business start-ups or those that are new to entrepreneurship or existing businesses who want to implement a new idea, make changes, get more clients, or expand their business.

Soccer Coaching For Dummies

So you are a brand new coach. What should I do? The court's long term goal is to prepare the player to successfully recognize and solve the challenges of the game on his or her own. What the game teaches children about how to live their life is much more important than any game will ever be. Keep the long weave in mind and how to teach them chapters that will last a lifetime. All of a coach all know that if male you may be to on these magnificent father feature in their child's life manager teacher facilitator understanding and identifying coaches must be cognizant of change debt a cure during the growth of their players coaches must recognize why players choose to participate in sport.

Coaches need to understand that their behavior has an effect on their player's performance and experience general characteristics of children. You seek a short attention span most individually oriented constantly in motion physically physically easily breezed genital characters the lack of children you seize physical coordination image here a hand and or a food coordination. Most media at best love to run, jump , roll and climb. Is it fair to you? Rapid Recovery mental development play consists of a high degree of imagination and content.

Activities tend to only be on the task at any time in problem solving stations. I'll say it's small bits of information at a time long scarce a game to your interests. Interest shows do not preset mental development in nature. Understanding of time and space relationship rules must be simple. Remember it can play children's games but children can't play adult games. Social development needs generous prize play without praise. You may verbalize the theme but do not understand grope up or call life to play our actions and pick our players Major. If parents give their children a toy adult, puzzle our train and start yelling at them while they play and read it. Do you think it would become a favorite toy getting Oregon's site to set up a theme there?

Registration forms medical release copies of roster are gamed pass league siege or recession rules. Game check laws of the game getting organized required equipment extra balls and a pump. Cars are beaks, whistle equipment, big beef or cheap t-shirts. First Aid Kit watch wait time or shop watch. Planning for the season. They've lobbied for coaching philosophy player development and coach development asked the question why am I coaching. Remember the final product is the person and not this game. Coaching your own child meeting with your own child before any team or parent meeting explains that you step out of the car there to change into a coach and they change into X soccer player coaching your arches. Explain to your child that you will treat them like every other player. Explain to your child that they must treat you like one after their teacher.

Keep the decisions in the car light and airy, don't begin coaching your child in the car. Ask them what they like best about the practice or what they might like to do. Next Practice preseason. Parents meeting discuss coaching philosophy and goals. Discuss what is expected of parents and players transportation communication sports mesh sheep coach player meetings collect information such as medical information parents skills inventory planning and running a practice. Do you love a plan that matches your players age and experience lies the k i s s principle when introducing native skills be organized and ball all hair air training plan. Failure to do so will only lead to confusion and discipline problems.

Typical youth seeking training can't exceed 60 minutes. Every child should have a bowl warm up at this moment. Education problems and soccer mistake games activities are mostly off. Everyone is deep along with some mace Games finish. Read three read trade games for small and the gods. No. G. Car you seek testicles fine this way or one way coaching activities checklist are the activities fun are the activities organized are the players involved in the activities it's crazy to end decision making being use and space use it props sheds no lines no labs no chapters and remember courts can often be more helpful by organizing less sane plans and allowing players the more game they be prepared to pay your line ups to ease your aim play against record playing type the role of the coach during game time is limited to making substations encourages players is strap on the I really needed teach them at air age to make their own decisions by YouTube for training from coaching during games remember to edge off your players don't.

All right Coach. It's not about winning it's about performing team management the game organization big game player Pierce's field reactions uniform choice player and evil time halftime location wars or injuries game degeneration Walter injuries endorsements no match Emily's risk management legal liabilities they get Soviet antiques complete 30 cured risk management from taking antiques head feed coaching clinic teeing off some consequence before you do it and seeing you never know how people are going to react you may in fact be liable. Risk management physical to take proper precautions to guard against post injury aggravation to provide proper equipment forward activity to provide a safe and appropriate training area Labor never leave a player long after training or games certain that players depart with their parents are assigned individual avoid being left alone with players who are not your children prevention and care of injuries first aid greed for the job coach.

Emergency Action Plan how and know how to use the following First Aid Kit ice and plastic bag for emergency use team safety and information cuts stay calm and praise your play. The department is savvy ABCs airway breathing insulation if necessary send someone to call 9 1 1 progression of injuries. Proper use of equipment prepare for shows prepare type of show for surface upkeep and monitoring of playing surface voids should leagues training during a heart as pre drills after day and then there is intense humidity ample water certainly and breeze to give players rest for rehabilitation of an injury period to return to play this term mined by a physical common a physical exam by a physical per year to participation know how to deal with common soccer injuries cuts and abrasions nosebleed bruises contusions sprains strains heat cramps heat exits his shin heatstroke fractures. These locations can cause use prevention and care of injuries. Always are on the side of caution before US aid and cpr reset feet. It called the incident and not all eggshells. YouTube and how the injured are cured follow up with a phone call. They cheered on the players commendation.

Coaching Motivates People

The little book of coaching motivates people to be Venus. Everybody's a coach in some aspect of their lives, and that means you, too. Coach two, we each letter stands for one of the five secrets of coaching, conviction, drive and never compromise your belief or learning practice until it is perfect. All of you will really respond predictably to performance. How does the base walk your talk commission, drive an effective leader, stand for something. Remember, if you don't stand for something, you will hold for anything.

The problem with most leaders is that they don't stand for anything. And yet leadership implies Smallman Towers something, a sense of direction. You cannot be a successful leader if you don't have a clear idea of what you believe. Why you are hated and what you are reeling. To go to the mat for beliefs and commissions for a while. The boundaries and direction that people want and need in order to perform those beliefs are what make things happen. Beliefs come true. And it is the leader's belief that is most important because they become self fulfilling. If I were with our beings it is a large part of life.

Thriver banks had good cause, providing the direction and concentration for Energis helping channel a force toward a single desired outcome. A war that is easy to achieve leads to the puzzle of Medoc three. Make sure everyone knows what the target is. Beans are a byproduct of hard work. Do you think you're doing your best everyday? Every week, every year. People must be prepared to perform to the best of their abilities so that they can aim for their targets. And you do that one day at a time. How can you do better than that? How can you be better than perfection, lady? When you heat your driving club, I'm for a specific spot on the fairway. If you miss that sport, you will probably still be one the fairways. But if you just aim for a buffet, that means that you will be there.

Our lady in big trouble without reason, the people perish. There are only those today. Must begin with a strong vision and a set of positive beliefs. That's part of it is that without them, the people they are courting not only laws but real bylaws, a clear reason and a set of operation failures. I really just had a picture of what things would look like if everything was running as planned and the reason was being fulfilled. It is exceedingly important for a leader of an organization to communicate his or her vision constantly to ensure that there is no doubt about the direction a team is heading. Success in life is forever and failure is not fatal. Don't get beat head way to win or get too down in the dumps when you lose. Keep things in perspective. Have your rebound. Form a seed bag. Speak volumes about who you are. Your attitude makes all the difference as a coach or a leader. Your own mental attitude towards winning and losing is Kay.

One of the marks of Frère success in life is to believe that there is a reason for everything. We can't control every Evans, but we can control our response to its character. Is its sum total of what you believe and how you act. Are you having me with people? It's just as important as ability. You need to have people of character who act according to the vision and values you believe in. You can't leave character to change. Wow. Who has mastered the art of leaving? Simply pursues his vision of excellence at whatever he does, leaving others to decide whether he is working or playing. The best coaches and managers in the world are those who absolutely love what they are doing. If you find you'll enjoy leading people to success, give it all you have got. If not, let someone else do it.

You can achieve greater success in your responsibilities as well. Either way, your mission statement keeps reminding you of your Pu's fusions while making important decisions regarding your career and your people. Over learning, effective leaders had their teams that practice sort of perfection. There is no easy walk to excellence. The best of the best now that there is no such thing as its heart cut. All agree the results are boiled on the foundation of practice and preparation. So get over prepared and help your people do the same. If you are going to compete today and be the best, you have to pass yourself and all that art. Today's leading organizations share a commitment to constant improvement. They believe they're going to be better tomorrow than they were yesterday.

Better next week than last week. Better next month than last month. And better next year than they were last year. The best way to continue to improve is to practice. It's not enough to tear up the steps. We must step up the stairs. The way leaders, coaches, managers, our parents, trade people is powerfully influenced by what they expect of people. People generally respond well to leaders who have high expectations and genuine confidence in them over learning. Cause people to perform. It's a higher level of expectation raising standards for everyone.

Thanks for coming, coach. How are you doing? Oh, okay. Listen, I need you in training camp and Julie on the field. Need you to go. You are going all the way this year. Goal setting is important, setting goals is important. But in most organizations, our end phase is this process and don't pay enough attention to what needs to be done each year. The goal is more important than setting goals is the follow up and attention to the time. The main four practiced perfection and all the things that spread teams that win from those that don't. It's the day to day process of observing and measuring your team's performance. That makes the critical difference in the end. Perfection happens. Only random Macanese are automatic.

The goal of Autoblog is to release people to do on their own what they're learning. Reflect where these goals and standards of the organization and to the career. For the rest of the time, the manager who has an organization full of individuals who operate out of guilt has no need to direct them because they are able to direct and monitor them, says. Practice does not make perfect, perfect practice, makes perfect people in organizations should develop a fascination with it. What's inferred? Every mistake should be noticed and corrected on the spot. There is no such thing as a small flavor that can be easily overlooked as a coach. If you let errors go unnoticed, you will ensure that more often will cure our Davilla Readdy. Effective leaders and the people and teams they coach are ready to change when the station demands it. In today's world, nothing stays the same.

The cheese is always moving. Many people are struggling right now because they haven't learned the power of flexibility. As a coach, you need to have those around you to become flexible.

From today Asiad that you are flexible enough to dare to need real things and help others to do the same. If your enemies per year Radim, if angry, irritate him. If you excel in a match fight, if not retreat and you do well, you'd better pay for a real Feodor plan and expect and read to change that plan. As a leader you must preserve the right to change plans. I haven't changed them at the last moment.

A system stays may dictate that option is not allowing yourself to give in to systems things it's loving. Those systems Thain's to give you success. Organizations that are constantly debating in a changing environment are making striking advances today. The ability of nimble organizations to transfer their Energy quickly in order to solve a customer's problem or meet their market. Southern need is the rare characteristic of being Oudeh Bill Readdy parading more. You need good ideas. And for week 30, many advisors' effective cards are continually scanning for data that will make their decisions more intelligent.

Good cards listen to their staff stuff, and once they've heard all of the important information, they are prepared to make the best decisions under any system. With many causes sellers are the wheels are in surprises, just new ways of doing what you already know what to do. Consistency. Effective leaders are pretty predictable in their response to peer firms with great courage. Treatment of individuals is predictable. Their focus is always on getting people to be their best if performance is going well. There are really two Brizes. But if a team or an individual isn't living up to the expectation they are ready to resurrect or reprimand, they behave in the same way again and again in similar systems. Thay's. It is not the mood they are in, but people's performance that distaste their response classes.

This is not behaving the same way all the time. It's behaving the same way in similar systems. Thay's. What we were talking about, this is the best fit kind of consistency, a consistency in responding to people's performance. Everything the coach canned, if she let little things go or not is cast, that often spells the difference between success or failure. Behavior is controlled by the consequence or is false. It receives them for consequence or responses people can receive are though they perform or do something. The most common is no response. The next most common response is negative. They get swept. Many managers are seen as single managers. They are not on until something goes wrong and then they fly in May. A lot of noise down on people and then fly out.

The last two Ryther actions and positive are the least used and yet most positive. When someone does something wrong. Ray Drake should focus his or her energy back. And what the original goal was a positive consequence is to feel calm. When a person does something right or makes progress and something positive follows good performers, they will want to repeat that good performance in the future. You can't catch your people doing something right. If you are not there to see them doing something right. In the typical organization, the most frequent response people get to their performance is Snorri's pass. Why? Because most managers are not around to see their people doing something right. Good coaching means being present on the spot, constantly giving a probe. Shared feedback on your team's performance. If you are going to take time to do the originals.

Be sure to take time to recognize what's important. If early words are positive, consequence is given. The person is apt to repeat the action. Positive consequences more to your future behavior. Recognizing good. Our performance is an important part of coaching. Today's leaders are too focused on doing but Arjun's to take time for what's important. Once leaders, coaches and parents see that prize and through coordination are greatly linked to performance, they will see them as integral parts of their job. After all, getting the best out of people, there is no such thing as a small mistake. Mistakes cannot be tolerated somehow. As a coach, you constantly hear to reiterate that your team backs trees.

Tom does for good performance and the reaction can be a powerful way to get people to day for schools. Their behavior after you deliver a pretty month. It's important for people to understand that we value them as human beings, harnessed, based, effectively they have high integrity and are clear and straightforward in their interactions with others. Cars operate out of all doubt in tranquility. They do not manipulate. They are sensory. If you remain true to yourself, you cannot be false to anybody else at the moment, you lose other people's trust. You lost everything. They were successful. And you have to work half days. You can work the first two halves and just kill 12. Never ask your people to do more than you are willing to do. A lot of leaders want to tell people what to do, but they don't provide a sample.

As a coach, your high standards of performance and passion to the time and people all depend on how hard you work. Set the stage for how your team performs. What people want most from us is us, or what we use or editors or perceptions. In the long run, it's not our skills or our know-how or our experience that makes the biggest impact. We are the main message. It takes a big person to admit to a mistake and then go out of his own way to right the wrong. A sense of who is simply a sense of who you are. A sense of humor helps you keep things in perspective. And more also permits you to accept criticism without getting consumed by it. And a lot of people in organizations today take themselves too seriously.

Without his sense of humor or we seem to stifle the child on others and ourselves. When all the emphasis in business is on whether we are doing things right or wrong, we never get to experience the light of exclamation. Isn't that interesting? Ballplayer's is temporarily respected in timeless ways. Being a great coach means sacrificing proctored and being alive for doing the right thing so that you are respected. In the long run, you will be buried as a better coach than whoever heads. The only way you can get prospects is to earn it. Has to bridge the gap between what we say and what we do. Effective coaches come from their people. Prize them since really the dregs reprimand them and beat Hopwood's a poor GI and ball all our hands with them. There are gaps in the main organization due to the difference between what managers say they stand for and how they actually treat people.

People with humility don't think less of them and say they think about themselves. Less greed, coaches, are not consumed by their own importance. Fear and the need to be right dominate people who are ego driven. Greed coaches want to win, but they don't fall apart when they lose. One of the most destructive traits a leader can have today is Arab lands. On the other hand, one of the best qualities a leader can have is to be in touch with his or her own vulnerability, believe in something bigger than is important. Daniel Fayad is eminently practical, and that was his source for Inner's stance. Read to S's. Today's leader, who will exercise it fed in something bigger than you is in a bear suit emotions.

It is an act to believe that requires you to step onto the field and walk your talk. The real difference in coaching is Balde believing in someone and then taking action to help the person be his or her best. Who believed in you for real? Difference in engorging is not about talent or personality or pride or ambition. It's about you believing in someone and then doing whatever it takes to have that person be his or her very best.

Executive coaching and MBC

Executive coaching and MBC I remember performance occurs if a person 's police station is important. All teams are reliable and necessary to stop trying to predict. Alison thinks you need to know first for a baseline value where your own assessment is a more important report. DB can be different from the true type. You may have different ideas of preferences at home and work creating awareness is the first step deep and straight. Most people confuse them. DB is sorted. Trade makes me sure that you can't have high tea or a stream.

J deep is about preference, trade is about behavior. Also Yancoal fiercest hysterical his story only the good the junk people's data don't know what the hell he saved my—. Breach starting taping the military most widely used edited fort the Como t looking for predictive instruments for dichotomies extroversion introversion sensing sink into team thinking feeling judged being pursued being scores indicate clearly to not degree for preference chaos for scarce are energizing how a person is energise perceiving whole person takes in information deciding how a person sides leaving lifestyle a person prefers one energizing how a person is energized extroversion preference for dreaming in energy from the outside world of people activities are teaching introversion preference for deriving energy from one's internal whirl of Ideas emotions or impressions to perceive wink while the person pays attention to sensing preference for using the senses to not tease what is real institutional preference for using the imagination to envision what is possible to look beyond the five senses don't call these unconscious person drink

3 deciding how a person decides thinking preference for organizing and structuring information to decide in a logical object away feeling preference for organizing and structuring information to decide interpersonal war you oriented way for leaving lifestyle a person prefers judgment preference for leaving empty land that an organization life perception preference for leaving a spontaneous and flexible life 1300 commonly to college students.

This is where today to tape not test the type rounded off E and F JS three persons E and F P down to persons E N T J two per cent E N T P five persons. E as if J ten persons e as if p nine persons E S T J seven persons E S T P six persons I N F J to a person i n if p six person I N T J one persons I N T B three persons I is f j Elm persons I s if be a persons I S T J ten persons I S T P five persons persons stage is c c Li programs and the services sate once thirties I gathered it is possible today as the original Myers brief story that these four Providence case R. R. Tobin now of one another some studies indicate they are indeed October know why all the studies seem to indicate that they are older than all with the exception of some observed manner correlation between the is and and the J peace case there is also a small gander shaved in the T FS K wait approximately six the persons of of males being F and sixty person of the males being t e i prefer it vocabulary extroversion e solubility t breads external ELC interaction expenditure of energy in dress.

In essence it was more to simply offer a tall ship introversion I territory. T the internal Tennessee Concentration. Concentration of energy and race in internal reaction limited through a lot of sheep as I preferred vocabulary sensing s expertise bass real realistic perspiration actual down to earth and salty fact practicality sensible air to show and harsh future speculated t inspiration possible head enclose fantasy function in JT imaginative T F preferred is vocabulary thinking t object to principles Poli Sci loves third iteration firmness impersonal just thighs categories standards could Itsuki analyze allocation feelings f subjects you rarely use sort your mail is a sense try and think Sir sums things instantly.

Tea Party Nation personal Hu main harmony good or bad are operation soon party awash in J P preferred vocabulary judgment. J SADLER decided feast planned hate round wants life closure decision making plan and complete the sigh wrap it up Argosy did lie get show on the road perception P pansy gather more data flexible adapt as you go let live happen. Open options your hand think open ended emergent Tante some think real time up there's plenty of time what date line let's wait and see the six same personality types the two preference for each of the four independents kids leave 60 unique combinations each combination being this single night air personality the commonly accepted ardor for describing each combination is given us energizing. E I attitudes attending s and perception deciding T F judgment leaving J P orientation S E and F J pay the gorge outstanding leader of graphs can be aggressive at having orders to be the best that they can be five person of the total population E and F P journalist uncanny sense of the motivation of others life is an exciting drama emotionally warm empathic five person of the total population E and T. J Field Marshall the basic driving force and need is to lead dads to seek a position of responsibility and enjoys being can execute to five person of the total population. E A.P. inventor and spastic in in everything and always sensitive to possibly this nonconformist. And in honor to five portions of the total population S E is f j seller most sensible of all types and nurturer of harmony outstanding—or hostesses 13 per cent of the total population. F SB interchange of radio TS attractive warmth and optimism smarty witty charming clever fun to be beat ready Genovese 13 person of the total population is T J.

Administrator much in touch with the external in the Romans way responsible pillar of strength is 13 Person of the total population is the DP promoter action rampages and things begin to happen piously composite two and three brainer offering users shock awake the get attention negative chants were par excellence 13 percent of the total population I NS I N F J other what awaited and full filed by having all those complex personality one person of the total population i n FP quests or high capacity for caring calm and pleasant face to the world high excise or horn or derived from intern no where use one portion of the total population. I am T.J. sciences most self confident and pragmatic of all the type position come very easily a boiler of systems and the airplane player of to hero Tico models warm person all the total population IN A.P. architect great inspiration in tone and language can really this Karen Condit action and inconsistencies the world X is preliminary to be understood one person of the total population I s I is if J Cause her words her desires to be of service and to minister to individual needs real loyal seeks Person of the total population I is if B is interested in the fine arts expiration paramilitary all action or art form the sense is arcane here then in order types five person of the total population I is D J thrust the deck I assume is impractical affairs guarding of time nor institution dependable seeks person of the total population I SDP artisan impulsive action life should be of impulse rather than of propose action is an end to itself feel is craves exist the moment more master of tools 5 percent of the total population the forecast abates to create MS. there are other systems that have been developed to model human personality the most well known and of to use one are those that divide human personality into form my your groups or temperaments hypocrites in and kills agrees describes the first four temperaments system also known as a four humors sanguine melancholy clearly and Craig Lam I teach more is silently Kersey and base took the six impersonated tips and categories guide them into four recognizable temperaments based on certain combinations of three off the force case as J is B empty and an F..

In addition then named each temperament after the Greek metal goalies you do figure who best exemplifies the world b as to boss of their temperament and if a poll of empty parameters use SJ A PERMIT choose is P. Dionysus and F. spirit ethics Apollo K focus on emotional need Sarge for S M or peace and harmony beliefs behaviors. How do I become the person I really am while you glued to your ship harmony with others can be very amiable the sightings but in pursuit need to live a life of significance. Search for your unique identity tends to focus on the good in others. A patiently impasse ever leeches anything that real elitists cherished role is managements that curtail his spokesperson and your guys ish spiritual style Augustin a. SiSense to erotica gay focused emotional need competence knowledge and are to lead and controls beliefs behaviors tries to understand whys of the universe weighty demanding of selves and others God sets her driver shorthand known and should have done better quality object to straight forward and logical indeed leaving you with others reluctance to state obvious legal redundancy in communications work is for improvement perfection proof alls kiss low off knowledge management that visionary Artie of systems move their spatial style Thomas a keenness as J that dirty commerce economic K focus emotional need responsibility tradition and are to maintain order beliefs behaviors call head again and tradition or establish who knew was really attentive to the tires believe in heroes she subordination and superordination rules commerce to be born and obligate my that is to serve give care save share shawls and ahs be prepared poster and great social units collapse church group name demands that traditionalists blazer consider the.

There's her spiritual style agony to use S.P. Joy artists dry eye cities gay focus emotional need freedom them independence spontaneity and art to have fun beliefs behaviors impulsive can be rarely expressive to do what I want when I want action to fulfill my current needs in pools not as embarrassment for longer term night works determined to coolly and quickly increases hungers for action without constraints tremendous stamina management style throb less hotter states are firefighters spiritual stat Francis of Assisi remember performance a cause of person blessed Tish an important.

All types are well able and necessary steps rank to parading adolescent type the enemy's height has leverage for debt coaches difficult to get easy to use. Use the orientation attitude here I show off use most concessions vs dominant explains great deal of behavior courting can see kindness and my your ease you debt is getting practically no attention in the management literature is the reality in many cases the chief a security officer does not have the concept show capacity to grasp the degree of complexity that he or she must now confront is short they supply the not know what they are really up against and what is happening to them and to their own nation let alone knowing what to do about it they simply can't absorb the range of information they shoot and organize it from multiple sources and focus it on the organization's problems in a way that holds both become reason and sore throats e.g.

Harry Levinson using deep in executed to coaching know your typology you are don't use it development concerns deep arenas of deep takes time notes I think deep of orders can help people misuse tape horribly don't toss around jangle keep it to yourself be careful with type intro words you seldom meet the general the author of The Lead to note W A S I and the way you a G uses energy coaching the intro words class system of principals in the bucks per Wade difficult to draw wild Sam shells contained building thrust overtime for accusing one team at a time a sir no conclusions only the big muddy if you're a surgeon why is extroversion so important deviance the dominant function dictates internal energy use you get Dick days internal attitudes dictates close or open system League days W A is I w a g Big D processing orientation coaching the extra words upon per Mabel easy to draw what's thrusting thinking out loud don't confuse sweet Congolese use external processing don't know what they think until they speak it.

Ah talk about it call for the bending style using tabbed in amusing quoting Annalise impact of function e I explore in phrases of J R B examine orientation to all the world contrast dinner meets with colleague use explorer impact of territory inferior functions create Portland t to discuss inferior these curves emergence of non preferred factions Annalise in Romans form the miles part remember performers eclairs a person lustration importance all tips are well able and necessary stop trying to operating and listen the age team and development team at various stages of development cognition and affection a cure simultaneously type and subject object who thought sheep subject. It requires organizing principle of experience object requires the compounds of an experience blind spots prey present are subject expertise coaches have people change their S O.

Coaching For Optimal Performance

Coaching for optimal performance is one characteristic of a good coach. Two elements of good coaching cesium 3 communication skills for effective coaching 4 5 steps of coaching for optimal performance 5 courting strategies for different behavioral style characteristic of good coach benefits of good coaching help develop employs competence at Couric unsatisfactory performance had the utmost performance problems forced through productive working full time a ship improving flow performance characteristic of good coach positive sporty goal oriented focus observance positive.

Your job is not critique mistakes finding failed in assessing blame in state your function is achieving productivity goals by coaching your staff to PE performance your job base coach is to get work case what they need to do day your up well including two's time instruction answers to questions and proc take action from outside into friends base your assessments on clear definable goals these specific task to dos Book communicate those goals to the people who actually have to do the work. Effective communication is specific and for accused you are far more likely to get action if Ted and blue leaves your office to focus on resolving the issue at hand. Being observant means more than just keeping your eyes and ears open. You need to be aware of what is in state as well. This is why if you are paying attention you won't have to wait for your sound bite to tell you about a problem bus and coach bus.

Thanks a lot Tess presume seats control others works on assembly keeps distant coach Lethem Elliott asks explorers seeks Commencement Challenge work beat takes responsibility makes context elements of good coaching cesium establish purpose established ground throbs. Keep focus. Develop a look. Speak clearly. This Cosmos PSP issue having clear proposals at the beginning of coaching cesium will enable you to conduct focus and productive ds. As with any meeting you and the employee you need to have a common understanding of certain factors.

The most important are timing roles. If you have lines to keep focus avoid making noise and think that distracts from the atmosphere. Don't look at your desktop or pee the a don't touch your papers don't answer the telephone it don't lounge into a man or look if you are coaching effectively your employers shoot. Probably the most of the talking. These tapes will help you communicate more effectively using the samplers. Most common terms Boyd the Chicago based best fake use the known to explain the unknown. Therefore in these you tend to limit the discussion to something manageable. You'll get other changes to discuss other concerns but only if you're to solve this specific concern right now.

Communication skills or effective coaching Salem communication principles for coaching one soft in the use. Or change it into. I took a ward sounding pushy is theater of your have to say Could you or would you be able to to focus on the solution not the problem. Instead we all might say we will pop down the shop walls and make three turn cans into cars instead of saying we can do that until next week say v B be able to do that next week. To take responsibility. Don't play blame instead. If it's not my fault. Say: Here's what I can do to fix that. 5. Say what you want not what you don't what is teed off. Don't drive too fast. Say drive carefully six Pocus on the feature not the past instead of I told you before not to say. From now on Salem shares information rather than air your acres are sealed off. No you are wrong. Say I see it like this gathering got information with your ex E..

Explore by asking a FEMA question to show you are listening and reflect your understanding. S silence. List them some more goodies some more effectively. Agents physically denied by the language helps us to focus on the speaker and encourage the speaker to give us more information. Etan's mentally follows the speaker's flow of thought. Listen to understand not a will you to listen first then. SS check it verbally for his face to clarify prob forager summary desires your understanding of good habits of effective listers. Looking at the speaker in order to observe body language and pick up the noise of speech asking questions gives the speaker's time to articulate their thoughts letting people first finish what they are saying before giving their opinion.

Remaining poised, calm and emotionally controlled looking alert and tested response could be noted and. Asking questions encouraging caesium. An effective question is brief and effective. Questions are focused and if two questions end in effect your questions constrict you briefly. The longer the questions the more likely you are to law it up in short sentences. It is just easier to understand. They are also easier to say to keep your questions brief. Think about two things. One. What do you want to learn from them? Answers to what BRS veal based Elie seed. This information focused on Taraji , this young girl and a particular aspect of that subject per question. If you don't you may render an answer man Inglis relevance.

Keep your questions on subject and on subjects even answers. Traces of the poison tactfully refocus calls are attractive. You need to accentuate the positive in your approach to questioning not because it makes you seem nicer but because your questions feel more effective than open questions. Open questions yield loss of information because they allow a person to explain what is most important or interesting and encourage elaboration probing questions probing questions and those that relate to the topic. We want to explore further. They encourage the speaker to flesh out the tires closed and open questions then let that happen once your trip is successful. Did you like the candidate? Did you have a good meeting that led up to that?

What did you manage to accomplish on your trip? In what ways do you think that candidates meet Ahmed? What happened at the meeting? Some probing questions. Can you be more specific? Can you give me an example of it? What happened then? For instance, how does this affect you? Well my cast did. Do you think you can fill me in on the details? Five steps for effective coaching. Describe your performance in a professional manner. Discuss the cause of the problem, identify and write down possible solutions. Develop specific action plan conduct follow up cesium described performance is you a professional manner as you describe the problem. Be specific. Point out the acceptable levels of performance and show the employee exactly where he is.

However all part doesn't meet those levels refer to any available that the dead will have indicated to his employ that there is a problem is important to open these discussions in a positive non-threatening way discuss the cause of the problem remain lax and friendly. Gather all the information you can about the problem by asking open ended questions. This question will bring in Q Closer to discharge the problem you may find it approach—to ask some specific questions designed to clarify and pinpoint causes. This is a good time to listen and respond with and seems to implore a expressed concern of frustration over fighters which he she feels cannot be controlled that noticing performance problems most performance problems are due to one or five factors or expectation ability shopped saying work and Roman's personal motivational problem role expectation.

Does the employee know what is expected? Thus she Even knows there is a problem. Ability. Does the employee have the requisite skills, abilities and aptitudes to perform the job. Has she. He is so trained to do a job job design that the employee has the necessary tools and resources to perform the job. Does the system's part good performance work? Enrollment is good performance rewarded or punished is poor performance rewarded it is the employee being treated fairly. The working conditions part good performance personal motivational problem that any use you or a problem X is in the employee's personal life that may contribute to poor performance is the employees attitude are moral preventing the employee from successfully applying his or her skills and abilities. Identify possible solutions after you have identified the likely causes of the performance problem.

You'll be bound to decide how to correct it. The employees glasses the problem so ask for his her ideas and write them down. This not only affects Heinz the employee's self esteem but it provides a write and record of possible solutions. The employer will be more committed to solving the problem if he she has had any say in the solution. Conducting follow up seizure in setting a date to meet again sends a message to the employee that solving the performance problem is important to you. It also tells the employe that you want to know how with he she's handling the action a great ball a follow up meeting enables you and the employee to get together to discuss and progress our problems and feel on of direction coaching strategies for different behavioral style for style of behavior dominance sadness influencing competence dominance they like the cultural they a remote by overcoming abrasion to accomplish the desired result they are direct forceful impatience and can be extremely demanding they enjoy being in charge and getting things done when they are negatively motivated.

Dan can be different. They don't like being told what to do. They are reluctant to do tasks that involve dealing with loss of detail. They will quickly become bored with a routine task. If Lansing. They like to shape the improvements by freelancing or proceeding orders they see things their way. There is life for handling complex tasks or working as long ranchers. They prefer to deal with people rather than things they enjoy making a federal impression. A good motivational environment and leaving people and environment optimistically will chat with you about anything on their minds. They motivate their people and love to generate answers. When negatively motivated they can be indiscriminately impulsive, steadfast in their life to cooperate with orders to carry out a task. They are a team player and prefer dealing with teams that want things at a time they are patient, reliable , loyal and resistant to sudden change in their inboard demands. They appreciate an orderly step by step approach. They tend to perform in a call system's predictable manner and pray for table harmony elsewhere.

And why Raymond Randall got them motivated. They can become stoppers as car moves usually express it in the form of passive resistance compress; they are cautious and demand quality and accuracy. They appreciate a portion is for trial careful planning. They are critical thinkers who are sticklers for detail. They prefer to spend time designing a station and lackeys' kidneys are slow to accept sudden change. They like following procedures and from that perv globally they all do respond favorably to logical well thought out plan options when they are negatively motivated. They become cynical or overly critical coaching strategies for dominance. Be clear, direct and to the point manual interact and communicate with them. Avoid being too personal and talking too much about non-work attempts. Let them know that you expect from them.

If you must write them, provide a choice that gives them the opportunity to make these errors, accept their need for reality and change when possible, provide new challenges as well as important. See the DZIEDZIC The force of others coaching strategies for influencing ask about things going on in their lives outside of Bourke. Let them share with you their Book at work and as were your objectives to their dreams and goals. Create democratic atmosphere and interaction meet them coaching strategies for said state dinners provide specific direction and offer as regime and necessary man implementing change.

Be sure to lay out a systematic step by step process and draw out their concerns and worries about the station. They need to feel secure and assure them that you have told Team to throw off before inserting change. You owe them a plan to deal with the problem and the cure. Coaching strategies for competence or fortune is for you to demonstrate their expertise. Plenty of times no time to prepare for meetings especially if they have an exam on the agenda to present station ideas to mitigate broach to contribute to long term success mentoring and coaching.

Coaching The Coach

Coaching the coach is more of a tutor absorbing your work and actions providing comments on execution and teaching skills which may be lacking. Coaches can come from the Main Source. A coach can be a colleague, a manager or an employee and doesn't have to come from the same faction or division in which you work, qualities of a good coach. Method of grading trainees as a coach. Mutually agreed Gough's review performance suggests change if any effective coaching includes good communication motivation.

Coach X is a model his possible coach a combination and Bert advantage while learning by doing to it Agassi's a one man not executing one day William Minds program exist three periodic emulation far useful in orientation of new execute to you and in developing by day two kids five class interaction between trainee and employer. There's an anxious one per pitch: your current manager deals with teams and practices to take years per year to be a good teacher and grades three bodies of daily routine for surface seemed time to make mistakes and learn from experience. For example, a coach may come from the company's personal training function. Some senior executives here and outside castle town to act as their coach. It is critical in the coaching of a sheep for the coach to have opportunities to observe your work and for you to respect the coach and be open to feedback. There is a vs breed use of change.

In organization use of coaching as a development tool has seen rapid growth in recent years. 77 percent of respondents reported that their organization's use of coaching has increased in the last five years. The mentor X as your counselor provides advice on career pets development opportunities and all where we know what it takes to become a leader in the company. He's a senior manager at least two levels above you in the organization. He must have broader experience in the company and the ability to place you into assignments that will help meet your development.

For example a publisher had a mentor when he first joined a large publishing company wants him to launch. He had lunch with his mentor, a senior wise priest in the company. He learned more about the publishing industry and how the company really worked at those lines than he could have in years if he had to discover all of it by himself. Why be a good mentor? Satisfaction in knowing you had an impact on someone's professional and personal development develops leadership skills and Boyd's confidence. A link with the younger generation gets a fresh perspective from you mentee victory's turns and increase proved that activity helped develop your professional network side.

Coordination from peers and superiors. A critical element in the mom talking role to a sheep is a mutual respect between you and your mentors qualities of a good mentor. A patient list Dinesh and Jill Eid who inspires trust Jesus advice without dictating actions and courage in the band says yes of her subpart offers contract to Katie's team as various complements open and harnessed a good role model to lift action and birds willing to spend time reach out and share an effective intermediary mentee an individual who is chosen or being a stagnant mentor by their organization. Qualities of a good mentee willing to be mentored and ask questions strive to give his her best. All the time I cease criticism. CHRIS softly learns from mistakes and has courage to try new things.

Accepts Responsibility: open and honest, respectful and grateful for what you learn. GROSS Why be a good man to one heaven. To help you. To me heartless to perfect from another person's experience. Three opens networks that would otherwise be closed for life long. Have faith in career advancement. Five practices for being a good mentor and mentor is like it too. It stays with you forever. Innovation and management development can take place in many forms, some deliberate by managers and some by intent now or Excel.

No coach or mentors. Robert D defines the different activities as follows guiding the process of directing an individual or a group along the paths leading from present day to inside state coaching how things in another person to improve awareness to set and achieve goals in order to improve a particular behavior you'll pay from this teaching. Having an individual or group develop cognitive skills anchor possibilities mentoring helping to shape an individual's beliefs and values in a positive way. Often a longer term career realtor or sheep from someone who has vanished before car selling had begun to improve performance by observing stations from the past. Both mentor and gain coaching must be viewed as long term.

Tall sheep are commented on two years to be obtained before drill or sheep are established. These two roles, whether performed by one person or two, are an essential ingredient in your career development. Conclusion coaching your employees will make you a better manager and a more valuable company employee and can only help you in your own career development. It is a part of my performance led culture of employment rather than the traditional employment model of job security. Both process and solutions Sweeting our time is an effective mechanism for enabling an organization to meet competitive pressures, plan for success and bring change. Thank you.

Coaching Mentoring

Learning object use up and completion of this chapter you will be able to define the key concepts associated with coaching and mentoring and you will be able to understand the basic process behind coaching and mentoring have so ability to introduce coaching and mentoring into the organization understand the benefits of courting and mentoring in the organization Learning Objectives Identify portions for coaching and mentoring.

Understand the nature of the internship that must be managed in any coaching or mentoring program used for knowledge for the overall benefit of the organization. Why do we need coaching and mentoring? Why do we need coaching and mentoring? The main reasons why organizations need coaching and mentoring activities are as follows: to maximize knowledge transfer the increase of skill levels forces session planning to maximize knowledge transfer coaching and mentoring price and learning channel that X Factor effectively transfers knowledge within the organization. Critical knowledge is maintained in the organization context and tool learning is evident.

The increased skill level the coaches and mentors can use to effectively transfer core skills customization of skills and abilities shown to the core activities of the business is retained. Cross training of staff can be achieved as Jason planning the ability for the organization to quickly break Condit's days and prepare them for new jobs is at hand by coaching and mentoring coaching and mentoring can ensure continuity of performance. One case staff leave the organization because core skills have been transferred. Ferries benefit carriers of coaching and mentoring that coach mentor to employ the department.

The organization benefits the coach mentor benefits through the coach mentor. Camp described job satisfaction. Further development of our skill level involvement in strategic activity model one understanding mentoring characteristic of our mentor task list. What routine art responsibilities of a mentor and discuss it. What does a mentor actually do in Anchorage? Call me sincere belief in per page ability. Those have said to give advice, give constructive feedback, and give formal and informal interaction.

The college's advice provides important things for the protegee to demonstrate his her skills, service career and lifestyle role model. S. meetings. Conference and other evidence together provide observation experience provide role playing experience a sea change discuss ideas co outsourcing challenges protest the end is seized with career planning and development emphasis on planning their will resumes cover letters provide sense of direction focus happen problem solving break ease combination interpersonal skills as is in career planning help said goals what about mantis potential to succeed capacity for self disclose serve willing to learn confidence to try new things communicate well to us others ambitious in turn focus off control hype shop investment where it is thrill to sheep sees through to a sheep between personal and professional growth.

Active learner focused therefore on but not have to please to mentor now silliness when to give Hap ethical takes into a team goal oriented organization time management skills open minded to one to mentor greatness test the mentoring readiness test one way you think about your development and Girl which of the following statements best represents floor beliefs a I am responsible for my own development and grow old. Ten B things change too fast. It is best to go with the flow. Five see if you were four. Good managers. They will take care of your Lord and love. Months 0 2.

What do you believe is the most effective role for mental a teaches me what may know. 5 B tell me what I need to do 0 c facilitates me crying, frying my tools and action. 10 3 When thinking about your expectation for romance or in clothes or sheep school day depends on what a mentor once I am and lead 0 b be clearly defined and communicated at the beginning of him in thawing relations she can see emerge as the relationship develops. 5 4 how aware you are of who all you are whilst you were you. The skiers and their lands that matter here are unique and your limitations. I am constantly trying to define and refine what I understand about myself. I saw some general impressions above myself. 5 See I haven't really thought about these things. Zero five. What do you feel the mantle should get out of their relationship?

A good feeling of having someone like me 5 B. Not much. They're already pretty successful and accomplished at what they do. Zero. See. They should learn as much from me as I do from them. Ten. Six. Which statement best represents your belief about plans and ideas. You and your mentor discuss a I will thing but this a long time before taking action. Zero. B I need to be willing to take action and put things into effect 10 C I will be willing to take action only men involved taking when a leader loses five sailors. How will you read feedback and observation from your mentor? A. Take my anger at the door, be open minded, willing to change and be clutch, then listen and take everything with a grain of salt. This is just one person's perspective. 5 see a sap those things that affirm what you know about yourself and reject that right your mentors doesn't understand the station you are dealing create 8 what should be your role in finding your mentor a thing up for a mentoring program and wait for the organization to assign you a mentor 0 b and mentor has to want to help you so Wade from them to ask you 5 see what for people who could help you and ask them to be your mentor. Ten nine.

What should be your responsibility in maintaining and mentoring a sheep? The sponsors of the mentoring program should define and monitor how often and for how long you meet zero. Be as boss words to keep in touch and require time for us to meet. Then I saw some entries giving me their time. They should define land and how often we meet 5-10 with statements. Best describes why you want to enter into a mentoring relationship. A I want to do all of my potential and career then be I would really like someone to listen to me and give you advice. One problem I am facing 5 C is kind of the thing you have to do in my organization and it sounds interesting. Zero. More due to mentoring the process. So you want to be a mentor or find a mentor. Step 1: Learn what mentoring is all about ; mentoring suggests and 3 make a match for Harry at our first meeting.

5 Do partnership cease hair as six month checkup. 7 continued personal graft aid concludes we do mentoring partnership. Step 1 Learn one mentoring is all about the mentoring partnership

is an agreement between two people sharing experiences and expertise to help with personal and professional graft. Step 1 Learn what mentoring is all about. To learn about mentoring you need to know what it takes to be a mentor. What does the mentor get out of it? What are the main tiers as possibilities? What does it mean to you? Get out of it. What does it take to be a mentor? Decide time reality check in the ratio. Carol development's plan.

What does a mentor get out of it based on successes practice ties interpersonal and management skills become recognized. Expanding their horizons gains more than demand does. What are the main tiers as possibilities willing to learn, able to say feedback willing to stretch, able to identify goals. What does it mean to get out of it? Listening to a reliable direction Gates fields in doors opened different perspectives. Step two: your mentoring suggestion, commit to one year in partnership, discuss no filed termination here, a six month checkup. Step three: make a match. You may be looking for a mentor and mentor for our boss. Step 3: make a match. General grade leads kids out of the chain of comment today to two great days.

Looking for a mentor. Look for someone at or near your location or use a mentoring program database looking for a mentee locates your location and send your people should reach out to junior people. Consider those who are quite not likely to ask for help or feel excluded. Step 4 Hey your first meeting may be in person by email or by phone. Discuss the mentee's expectations. Choose a natural setting face to face. This car's value will need to and how often discussed when it is or can't form agreed confidence. Yearly get to know each other. Step 5 continued the partnership mentor be use listening counseling coaching career and rising and goal setting to have mentee develop in the ways your care your developments play identified.

Fill in the gaps explained away edible options explorer referral resources with staff is the theme ever laid. Each meeting step seat has a six month checkup. This great progress review of your development plan. Ask questions step seven. Continuing with personal growth in training can expand. All love bald bad tennis. Mentoring can help people become more comfortable with differences. Resources to have gender differences ethnic differences personality differences Sep. I conclude the mentoring partnership. Many partnerships continue not to notify. If you decide to end it early, give it a shot. Review and revise Gore's express gratitude.

chapter 3. Identifying or portrait Ts for courting and mentoring definitions. What does the term coaching mean to you? What does the term mentoring mean to you? Coaching mentoring. Sighs slur sir. Discuss angry white coaching and mentoring. I'm not micromanaging. Just for superstars boredom meant what coaching and mentoring are instead of being seen as a low level add on activity. Coaching is a core competency necessary for knowledge transfer instead of being seen as a privilege for Black you feel entering is a two way process of delays and planning people helping each other to find their way on the job in the organization and over a lifetime. Baldrick here observation dialogue and agreement target it at building individual and team cup ups abilities the force of continuous improvement in organization coaching and mentoring hall of shame.

Take a moment and record one or more horror stories from your own personal expertise or that of others in clusters of two and three people. Briefly describe some of these experiences. Select one for NL is using the NL is sheet now reflect on an example for excellent coaching and mentoring either more being you or someone as is you think about this station. What work rather. What factors can't far success coaching and mentoring meet groups stage in group Development forming storming norming and performing stage show leadership. I think my dating coaching and mentoring coaching and mentoring. A final question. Sure coaching and mentoring folk song content process rationale case 31 the story four roles lean yellow model for making in book. What are the different types of mentoring is important to understand.

There are several types of mentoring: natural mentoring sessional mentoring supervisory formal facilitator mentoring natural mentoring natural mentoring occurs all the time and always has it happens ran on person reach out of order and a career happening relationship develops is served shores. This type of mentoring most often occurs between people who have a lot in common. This is because they are usually more comfortable with those who are most like ourselves in situational mentoring stations and mentoring is usually short lived and happens for a specific purpose.

An example would be when one worker has another lead and knew of his computer systems or man sometimes was on an informational interview with someone who is in a carrier they are considering supervision and mentoring meeting partners. L good spur Rieser mentor their subordinates throwbacks may not be a subject matter expert here really task called foreplay was far more vessel and mentoring formal vessel date mentoring programs are tractor programs in region organization mage mentors with mentees. They made Padgett a special segment of the organization whose character development may be lagging behind that of orders to have that group advise further they may sign mentors mentees and monitor the process of mentoring connection.

Example of the mentoring program part of formal part informal use benchmarking and research programs are most successful my mentee selects mentors email partnership I relabel chose a user friendly program available to all educate people saw Davie from mentoring partnership includes a database of food and chairs where best thing people can sign up as mentors and or search for mentors more useful for those who can find a mentor at that location. Case study to the kids dilemma chapter 5 understanding coaching. What is coaching? There is some confusion about what exactly coaching is and how it differs from other happening behaviors such as counseling and mentoring.

Broadly speaking, coaching is defined as developing a person's skills and knowledge so that their job performance improves, hopefully leading to the achievement of organizational objectives. It targets high performance and improvements at work. Although it may also have an impact on an individual's private life it usually lasts for a short period and focuses on specific skills and Goss characteristic of coaching in organization. It is essentially a non directive from off developments a focus on improving performance and developing individual skills personalities use may be discussed but the emphasis is on performance Edberg coaching activities handball organizational it and in the regional Goss assumes that the individual is psychologically larger and does not require a clinical integration provides people with feedback on what their strengths and their weaknesses.

It is a skill base activity developing a coaching culture as one coaching is the proud dominance deal of managing and working together and their commitments to improvement. The organization is embedded in a party that is committed to improving the people whose coaching is dealt with by external coaches full time and part time internal coaches who may be line managers or members of the eight hour departments helpful to enable internal and external coaches to share supervision arrangements. These and ABA's external cautious forget get a better understanding of the organization and also enables them to share their perspectives on what is happening within the organization.

Coaching spur vision coaching can be a challenging and lonely activity. Coaches need structured apartment teams to reflect on their practice. Such important things can have cause continuously to develop their skills as well as provide them its part. It can also be an important quality that surrounds activity for organization and as Sarge of organizational learning about issues being addressed in coaching season's stakeholders in coaching the privilege of the relationship is between the college and the individual. Other case stakeholders include the person representing the organization interest age practitioner and the individual manager. Both of these parties interested in empowering the individual's performance and therefore the contribution to the organization made is coaching the best development in termination.

First step identification of some kind of learning or development needed either by the individual themselves, their line manager or someone from the eight hour departments. Next step is for the manager and the individual to decide how best. The need can be met then is coaching the best of Loughlin integration. Coaching is just one of a range of training and development integration to meet identifying learning and development needs should be cost alongside other types of the allotment interactions.

Employee preference should also be borne in mind. There is a danger that coaching can be seen as a solution for old canes. Often Lockman needs examples where coaching is suitable to have been a competent technical expert. Develop better interpersonal or managerial skills though loping an individual's potential and providing care is part. Developing a more strategic prospect to offer a promotion to a more senior role handling conflict stations so that they are so effectively important. Remember that. Here are some individuals who may not respond that the coaching may be because their problems are best. Deal with it. Why?

In order, type of interaction or maybe because the institute may interfere with the effectiveness of coaching. So therefore coaching has begun. Organizations need S's and the ratios readiness. Some examples of stations when coaching is not an appropriate diversion. Ah if the individual has physical Yoko problems they are resistant to coaching. Are they a leg stand in sight? Case that these three interesting ads Poor Duke University thank you and good luck.

Coaching Psychology

End in probing performance roads. Me coaching why and how. Grow and similar modus. Is there more to coaching than growth? The psychological underpinnings of coaching tree frameworks practical tools reflection. Why improved effectiveness increased practical skills. Increasing resumes under praise enables a focus on the outcomes, increases decision making and personal effectiveness increases self awareness. Coaching is unlocking a person's potential to maximize their own performance.

It's having them to learn rather than teaching them to grow . We'll really keep options for the underpinning questions. Gee what is it you are trying to achieve? What does that look like? How will you know why you have achieved the goal? Do you know what is happening at the moment in relation to this goal? What is a realistic deadline for achieving the goal? Oh What opinions do you have? What can support you to achieve this goal? What information training do you need? W what is the first step that you need to take towards this goal. How much weight do you have to achieve this goal? What small action really you take when you lead this seizure. Other mothers Strong t grow any others. Some of the basic skills report engagement delivering messages listening skills questioning skills process skills self awareness psychology and coaching.

Illegal exercise spanned four five means reading the story and answering the 18 statements with two falls and down now add up the subtotal for each clown. Be prepared to share those results. There is no one in our right world if we don't see the world as it is. We see the world as we are. More on perception rational analytical side addressing process Shin's mental models that people have about the world feelings and emotional about the world and about chance that they have identified in their heads a curing the specific skills and capabilities to succeed in applying new practice behaviors and process that is psychological frameworks dished out existence shill perspective cognitive behavioral salvation is produced feeds bowels and get that whole awareness in the moment but turns of behavior told in coaching sessions are mirrors of patterns outside Cecil's mindful interactions and enticing at avert a pattern a position to achieve work.

Meta mirror failed experiments exploit and explore the site's call senses cognitive behavioral therapy. There are three core ideas we hold about the world that underpin our thinking pattern: our belief about the world leads to the station's specific responses that we need or choose. We think like this because I have three core beliefs. I must be perfect. If I don't do well then it is therefore leading to stress anxiety depression shame and guilt others must like me. If you don't then you deserve to be punished leading to anger, passive aggressiveness and boilers. Life should be easy. If not I can't stand it leading to self other pity for all stressed nation addicts. Your behavior depresses your thinking errors and specific thinking patterns that lead to station specific automatic negative tools including all or nothing taking magnification minimization personalization emotional is usually a solid mind reading labeling.

This call team the positive demanding ness focusing on the negative. Fortune telling overgeneralization I can't stand. It is to blame. What does this mean? People are not disturbed by Evans but by the we. They take off then everything is bad. What your opinion makes it and that opinion lies within yourself. HAMMETT why then there is no one to you for. There is nothing either good or bad but thinking makes it so the good people can learn to notice and change their own polls with powerful emotional and behavioral benefits. The psychological management model activating Evans B believes C consequences. The dispute is an effective technique, his thinking skills are career realistic , major reading techniques, self acceptance, exercise , hard work and practice common statements. The director makes me so angry. Billy gives me panic attacks, company politics make them furious, giving chapters makes me feel dreadful, makes an error or makes me useless.

My Burke Lord makes me feel so depressed about investment fund manager Pete's. This is a complete waste of time. I'm not a party slur. This is terrible. I will be seen as the junior guy who's just come along for experience pets. I can do these. I am good at this. The implication of making game mistakes is not so bad. Just because I have made one mistake it doesn't mean I am entering the Joe clamber seats. I am going to die. This wasn't in the game played. This shouldn't happen to me. I can't sit here hoping for things to get better sets. It is a feat to ban five years old who wants to clean the world, look back and realize how scary denied had been.

Could be sitting here for days. Have to keep making decisions. If you don't. There is no hope. Did Not end note at the end of the rope. Then it will be quick. You haven't even started to make it's miles and miles and on really bad ground sets it to me that I should set definite targets. I can get to that cold way in two and. Exercise. Focus on one aspect of your performance that you'd like to improve. Examine the tools that might be inhibiting your performance. Write this down in the left hand club to challenge this. I. They legalistic logical half foot write down any performance enhancing tools in the right hand.

Club solutions focus. Part one in pairs decides who is a and b b, think of a time value where at your base and spend three minutes describing it to get as much detail as possible. Observe wayBill positive concrete details listen carefully to and not what your partner says. What was it about the moment that made it sparkle for you? What do you remember most about yourself? At that moment but might others have not aside what did others say do what else sparkling moments. Part Two giving air fumes identifying resources based on what your partner has just said reflects on what you know now about their excellent qualities, skills and resources as a personal team for a moment then tell them and wait for them to say thank you.

Sparkling moments but three fine small actions based on the decisions you have so far A asks B chose a small action that will increase the likelihood of more sparkling moments happening at work in the following days and weeks. Make sure the action is small and specific solutions philosophy problem stuff creates problems solely shouldn't create solutions bringing coaching and psychology together psychologically based tools and techniques are used everyday by courts and managers and individuals to end Hanes' performance and effectiveness.

The tools and techniques discussed here today can be easily applied psychological understanding is particularly helpful for coaches ethical practice working to improve individual performance at work can take unexpected directions. Whatever tools and techniques please use there are boundaries too. Competence refers to a psychologically trained and more experienced coach, a counselor or territories is the best next step.

Coaching Psychology Part 2

End in probing performance roads. Me coaching why and how. Grow and similar modus. Is there more to coaching than growth? The psychological underpinnings of coaching tree frameworks practical tools reflection. Why improved effectiveness increased practical skills. Increasing resumes under praise enables a focus on the outcomes, increases decision making and personal effectiveness increases self awareness. Coaching is unlocking a person's potential to maximize their own performance.

It's having them to learn rather than teaching them to grow . We'll really keep options for the underpinning questions. Gee what is it you are trying to achieve? What does that look like? How will you know why you have achieved the goal? Do you know what is happening at the moment in relation to this goal? What is a realistic deadline for achieving the goal? Oh What opinions do you have? What can support you to achieve this goal? What information training do you need? W what is the first step that you need to take towards this goal. How much weight do you have to achieve this goal? What small action really you take when you lead this seizure.

Other mothers Strong t grow any others. Some of the basic skills report engagement delivering messages listening skills questioning skills process skills self awareness psychology and coaching. Illegal exercise spanned four five means reading the story and answering the 18 statements with two falls and down now add up the subtotal for each clown. Be prepared to share those results. There is no one in our right world if we don't see the world as it is. We see the world as we are. More on perception rational analytical side addressing process Shin's mental models that people have about the world feelings and emotional about the world and about chance that they have identified in their heads a curing the specific skills and capabilities to succeed in applying new practice behaviors and process that is psychological frameworks dished out existence shill perspective cognitive behavioral salvation is produced feeds bowels and get that whole awareness in the moment but turns of behavior told in coaching sessions are mirrors of patterns outside Cecil's mindful interactions and enticing at avert a pattern a position to achieve work.

Meta mirror failed experiments exploit and explore the site's call senses cognitive behavioral therapy. There are three core ideas we hold about the world that underpin our thinking pattern: our belief about the world leads to the station's specific responses that we need or choose. We think like this because l have three core beliefs. I must be perfect. If I don't do well then it is therefore leading to stress anxiety depression shame and guilt others must like me. If you don't then you deserve to be punished leading to anger, passive aggressiveness and boilers.

Life should be easy. If not I can't stand it leading to self other pity for all stressed nation addicts. Your behavior depresses your thinking errors and specific thinking patterns that lead to station specific automatic negative tools including all or nothing taking magnification minimization personalization emotional is usually a solid mind reading labeling. This call team the positive demanding ness focusing on the negative. Fortune telling overgeneralization I can't stand. It is to blame. What does this mean? People are not disturbed by Evans but by the we. They take off then everything is bad. What your opinion makes it and that opinion lies within yourself.

HAMMETT why then there is no one to you for. There is nothing either good or bad but thinking makes it so the good people can learn to notice and change their own polls with powerful emotional and behavioral benefits. The psychological management model activating Evans B believes C consequences. The dispute is an effective technique, his thinking skills to career realistic major read techniques, self acceptance, exercise , hard work and practice common statements. The director makes me so angry. Billy gives me panic attacks, company politics make them furious, giving chapters makes me feel dreadful, making an error or makes me useless.

My Burke Lord makes me feel so depressed about investment fund manager Pete's. This is a complete waste of time. I'm not a party slur. This is terrible. I will be seen as the junior guy who's just come along for experience pets. I can do these. I am good at this. The implication of making game mistakes is not so bad. Just because I have made one mistake it doesn't mean I am entering the Joe clamber seats. I am going to die. This wasn't in the game played. This shouldn't happen to me. I can't sit here hoping for things to get better sets. It is a feat to ban five years old who wants to clean the world, look back and realize how scary denied had been.

Could be sitting here for days. Have to keep making decisions. If you don't. There is no hope. Did Not end note at the end of the rope. Then it will be quick. You haven't even started to make it's miles and miles and on really bad ground sets to me that I should set definite targets. I can get to that cold way in two and. Exercise. Focus on one aspect of your performance that you'd like to improve. Examine the tools that might be inhibiting your performance. Write this down in the left hand club to challenge this. I. They legalistic logical half foot write down any performance enhancing tools in the right hand. Club solutions focus.

Part one in pairs decides who is a and b b think of a time value where at your base and spend three minutes describing it to get as much detail as possible. Observe wayBill positive concrete details listen carefully to and not what your partner says. What was it about the moment that made it sparkle for you? What do you remember most about yourself? At that moment but might others have not aside what did others say do what else sparkling moments. Part Two giving air fumes identifying resources based on what your partner has just said reflects on what you know now about their excellent qualities, skills and resources as a personal team for a moment then tell them and wait for them to say thank you.

Sparkling moments but three fine small actions based on the decisions you have so far A asks B chose a small action that will increase the likelihood of more sparkling moments happening at work in the following days and weeks. Make sure the action is small and specific solutions philosophy problem stuff creates problems solely shouldn't create solutions bringing coaching and psychology together psychologically based tools and techniques are used everyday by courts and managers and individuals to end Hanes' performance and effectiveness.

The tools and techniques discussed here today can be easily applied psychological understanding is particularly helpful for coaches ethical practice working to improve individual performance at work can take unexpected directions. Whatever tools and techniques please use there are boundaries too. Competence refers to a psychologically trained and more experienced coach, a counselor or territories is the best next step.

Coaching Skills

Coaching skills for high impact teaching the day one education coaching. It's in a big room or school teacher and popular performances. Two essential coaching skills for the classroom. 3 developing the micro skills of teaching for structuring effectively from five top tips. Season 1 education coaching has an impact on what school teacher and pupil performance was school culture. Some opening assumptions for school culture. Good teaching is a set of learnable skills not a God given gift.

Performance management is about mutual performance. Encourage experimentation and occasional disasters. We should be intolerant of mediocrity, a genial immoral culture boys reflection. Real change comes from meeting heavy clear we've all thought these social skills of teaching to storing behavior are to make them out with everything else around them. Big performance will happen. Value pairs meet your imagination, study , explore and grow. Motivation is straining our probe that means the creative means to decide or expect the best plan and work for the best.

Whatever you do in life you are going to work hard for it. So you might as well choose to work hard for what you really love and want to do. Education means awareness and use of what works. Teens' debt woes have a pattern and this can be learned through all holy and applied caesium to essential classroom coaching skills. Listening while dealing and taking this performance coaching to raise puppies inspires techniques for changing overcoming barriers, learning so show that people who have achieved success in different walks of life head prey solely for 18 goals. Outcomes smart why that's goal setting work.

We'd sing and behave in a way consistent with our beliefs. Get Pappas to write down the cause and review them regularly the rate killer actor rating systems thoughts comfort zone body of beliefs and attitudes particular activating systems and observation told from us and s dark feeling and emotions techniques for change positively in listing and reflection. A simple strategy to reinforce positive beliefs those feelings and reception reframing a powerful strategic war changing negative feelings and the effect on performance create powerful anchors is expressive. Holding forums pattern breaking imagination and natural ability to bring to mind what is seen, heard and felt rational analysis and objective analysis of objects.

Learning dialogue music and symbols emotional barriers and solution negative memories. Negative expectations project negative expectations of their future and the meeting belief in a pro reads Martians. Other damaging thought patterns and barriers: jealousy , serviceable take on the real estate competitiveness, mindless gossip and lack of discipline judgment title believes in editors indicate desire means programming for positive results. Self-confidence in high self esteem.

Goal setting for desired outcomes using a solution focused approach or systematic approach to math harmed outcome. The magic of cost setting is to show that people who have achieved success in different walks of life and have praised written goals are well formed outcomes. SMART WHY DOESN'T goals set and are waiting and behave in a way consistent with our beliefs.

Get partners to write down goals and review them regularly caesium 30 then developing the microscopes off teaching part 1 creating a s in relation culture curl of his Gibbon get that into school life without necessarily doing anything with it.

John Mack beats me short measure what we were you not value what we can measure David Reynolds aim to be a high credibility organization such complex social organization as air traffic control towers continuously round the risk of the Astros and obviously acceptable failure of the public world he really discounts several thousand concept to his days of patiently monitoring and controlling two way crowded sic is always Chicago or London if two jumbo jets were to co-lead or either city throw fog snow computer systems failures and fear B tornadoes in spite of thousands of flies per day in buses keys such a collision has never happened a ball any city a remarkable live a low performance ability Michael to us in the say on of the most high play the Kate nations on earth is weight in any group of Honduras.

To this beginning first grade in a particular year approximately 16 will not have obtained either the high school diploma or a general education the law looks out for date birth are thirty years later. In butane just under half of all 60 year old poppies will not pay off the benchmark of five or more high grade public extermination packs in the national system. Obviously many nations have ever lower levels of educational performance therefore for me these coaching is about teacher deals last month. It's also about stubborn entitlement to good teaching forms of self education students performance that results targets us at our starter quiz show memories and focus groups faculty we in observations she's Blas building these is genuinely self immolation talking point How might use this approach in your own school the essential skills of good teacher talking point.

What do you think are the three most important ingredients of a good teacher and bet? How to customize these for your school. How to spell out the essential skills explicitly lady's size so observation. She's hard to develop a shared approach to observation protocols and specific eases as focus using observation traits questions rather than comments. How do you feel about the chapter learned? Why did you start the race with X tricky x. How many students do you think took part in the disease shows value because of boys or girls' efforts? Why did you stand like you did for Looper? They have to provide different training.

What are the good features of coaching in your school? 2 How mad do you articulate a share of all effective learning and teaching. 3 how they ensure consistency across teams for how they do love the teaching skills of people at different faiths. 5 What are your points for action sessions for understanding and structuring effectively since using coaching to improve behavior, personalized learning and coaching. Making it work in your classroom. What do we know about effective behavior management? Young people dating of nothing but terms have no reference for parents or old age. Some principals' good behavior management is a prerequisite for effective teaching and learning.

Again we can identify what effective teachers do. We shouldn't tiptoe around these; you are a heavy focus on systems that can create problems. Keep it simple and light. Don't use case studies, teachers and masters take a long term approach, not quick hits. Let me know from research into behavior management practice schools have one of the world's working assumptions: if mild punishment is not pro-effective, then racial strife is more severe punishment. In other words one is led into a false escalation rather like the postcard. Notice the beating will continue until more it improves they will love a hostile before. Set out. Model the behavior and language you expect after giving this choice to avoid the public arena by being prepared to defer use of talking points.

What are the implications for your own school learning performance strategies? Promoting positive communication or report developing self esteem increasing motivation setting learning goals and the steps to get there. Performance cause right now raising achievement is keyframing positive expectation giving immediate and positive feedback listening questioning modeling thinking skills making learning can't carry your hobby and life goals existence wake group work learning to kids. Promoting recognition and responsibility for each pupil's learners creating interesting and meaningful activities. Mind Map gangs providing more choice use curiosity anticipation promoting active reflection since your five top tips for effective coaching the coaching process creating a coaching culture Top Tips coaching one talk with them endlessly using insight gained or modify your view to a sheep expectation and chapter to be genuinely interested in your purpose.

3 Learn alongside your pupils. Treat them as a couple, learn and prepare your chapters and as you would if you were going to coach your team to win every time. 4 You must have a very high

expectation of all your pupils and replace all negative judgments out attitudes with a positive alternative and just so and calm and accurate to an observation. 5 defeat and focus on your coaching goals. Use you is to set up a desire for learning something new every day also and not how you did it. Identify your learning pay their top tips a coaching culture sees staff from your students entitlement to God teaching 7 both a culture of constants ongoing evolution a process a strong emphasis on self immolation might develop a child leave off the essential skills teachers need then develop a hostile to develop then and relentlessly aim for. Carson simply.

Conclusion

End in probing performance roads. Me coaching why and how. Grow and similar modus. Is there more to coaching than growth? The psychological underpinnings of coaching tree frameworks practical tools reflection. Why improved effectiveness increased practical skills. Increasing resumes under praise enables a focus on the outcomes, increases decision making and personal effectiveness increases self awareness.

Coaching is unlocking a person's potential to maximize their own performance. It's having them to learn rather than teaching them to grow . We'll really keep options for the underpinning questions. Gee what is it you are trying to achieve? What does that look like? How will you know why you have achieved the goal? Do you know what is happening at the moment in relation to this goal? What is a realistic deadline for achieving the goal? Oh What opinions do you have? What can support you to achieve this goal? What information training do you need? W what is the first step that you need to take towards this goal.

How much weight do you have to achieve this goal? What small action really you take when you lead this seizure. Other mothers Strong t grow any others. Some of the basic skills report engagement delivering messages listening skills questioning skills process skills self awareness psychology and coaching. Illegal exercise spanned four five means reading the story and answering the 18 statements with two falls and down now add up the subtotal for each clown. Be prepared to share those results. There is no one in our right world if we don't see the world as it is. We see the world as we are.

More on perception rational analytical side addressing process Shin's mental models that people have about the world feelings and emotional about the world and about chance that they have identified in their heads a curing the specific skills and capabilities to succeed in applying new practice behaviors and process that is psychological frameworks dished out existence shill perspective cognitive behavioral salvation is produced feeds bowels and get that whole awareness in the moment but turns of behavior told in coaching sessions are mirrors of patterns outside Cecil's mindful interactions and enticing at avert a pattern a position to achieve work. Meta mirror failed experiments exploit and explore the site's call senses cognitive behavioral therapy. There are three core ideas we hold about the world that underpin our thinking pattern: our belief about the world leads to the station's specific responses that we need or choose.

We think like this because 1 have three core beliefs. I must be perfect. If I don't do well then it is therefore leading to stress, anxiety , depression , shame and guilt. Others must like me. If you don't then you deserve to be punished leading to anger, passive aggressiveness and boilers. Life should be easy. If not I can't stand it leading to self other pity for all stressed nation addicts. Your behavior depresses your thinking errors and specific thinking patterns that lead to station specific automatic negative tools including all or nothing taking magnification minimization personalization emotional is usually a solid mind reading labeling. This call team the positive demanding ness focusing on the negative.

Fortune telling overgeneralization I can't stand. It is to blame. What does this mean? People are not disturbed by Evans but by the we. They take off then everything is bad. What your opinion makes it and that opinion lies within yourself. HAMMETT why then there is no one to you for. There is nothing either good or bad but thinking makes it so the good people can learn to notice and change their own polls with powerful emotional and behavioral benefits. The psychological management model activating Evans B believes C consequences. The dispute is an effective technique, his thinking skills to make realistic major reading techniques, self acceptance, exercise , hard work and practice common statements. The director makes me so angry. Billy gives me panic attacks, company politics make them furious, giving a chapter makes me feel dreadful, makes an error or makes me useless.

My Burke Lord makes me feel so depressed about investment fund manager Pete's. This is a complete waste of time. I'm not a party slur. This is terrible. I will be seen as the junior guy who's just come along for experience pets. I can do these. I am good at this. The implication of making game mistakes is not so bad. Just because I have made one mistake it doesn't mean I am entering the Joe clamber seats. I am going to die. This wasn't in the game played. This shouldn't happen to me. I can't sit here hoping for things to get better sets.

It is a feat to ban five years old who wants to clean the world, look back and realize how scary denied had been. Could be sitting here for days. Have to keep making decisions. If you don't. There is no hope. Did Not end note at the end of the rope. Then it will be quick. You haven't even started to make it's miles and miles and on really bad ground sets to me that I should set definite targets. I can get to that cold way in two and. Exercise. Focus on one aspect of your performance that you'd like to improve. Examine the tools that might be inhibiting your performance. Write this down in the left hand club to challenge this. I. They legalistic logical half foot write down any performance enhancing tools in the right hand. Club solutions focus. Part one in pairs decides who is a and b b think of a time value where at your base and spend three minutes describing it to get as much detail as possible.

Observe wayBill positive concrete details listen carefully to and not what your partner says. What was it about the moment that made it sparkle for you? What do you remember most about yourself? At that moment but might others have not aside what did others say do what else sparkling moments. Part Two giving air fumes identifying resources based on what your partner has just said reflect on what you know now about their excellent qualities skills and resources as a personal team for a moment then tell them and wait for them to say thank you. Sparkling moments but three fine small actions based on the decisions you have so far A asks B chose a small action that will increase the likelihood of more sparkling moments happening at work in the following days and weeks.

Make sure the action is small and specific solutions philosophy problem stuff creates problems solely shouldn't create solutions bringing coaching and psychology together psychologically based tools and techniques are used everyday by courts and managers and individuals to end Hanes' performance and effectiveness. The tools and techniques discussed here today can be easily applied psychological understanding is particularly helpful for coaches ethical practice working to improve individual performance at work can take unexpected directions. Whatever tools and techniques please use there are boundaries too. Competence refers to a psychologically trained and more experienced coach, a counselor or territories is the best next step.